Financial

Legacy

Niyi Adeoshun

Financial Legacy

8 Lessons My Father Taught Me about Money

Nukan Publishing

Financial Legacy
(8 Lessons My Father Taught Me About Money)
by Niyi Adeoshun
http://www.niyiadeoshun.com

Copyright © 2016 Niyi Adeoshun

ISBN: 978 1 530 15377 0

Published by **Nukan Publishing**

First Printed in UK 2016

Cover designed by **Design2Impact.co.uk**

Notice of Liabilities

The Publisher has strived to be as accurate and complete as possible in the creation of this book, notwithstanding the fact that he does not warrant or represent at any time that the contents within are accurate due to the rapidly changing nature of the financial world.

This book is not intended for use as a source of legal, business, accounting or financial advice. All readers are advised to seek services of competent professionals in legal, business, accounting, and finance fields.

"The core of any family is what is changeless, what is going to be there -- shared vision and values."
-   Stephen R. Covey

"The legacy of heroes is the memory of a great name and the inheritance of a great example."
Benjamin Disraeli
(British Prime Minister. 1804-1881)

Endorsements

An intriguing father to son relationship that brought out the most amazing financial education of all times. As an international businessman it is remarkable to see a book that has the core foundation blocks of success and financial prosperity written with such a simplicity and very concise.

It is compelling, informative and contains undeniably provoking truths to shape and reshape the mind of future entrepreneurs and all that desire to be successful. It is a 'must have' for parents and children.

Chinedu Onyemobi
Director, Corlet Professional Ltd, London, UK

I am proud to say the author of this book is my elder brother. He taught me how to read novels like James Hadley Chase, Sidney Sheldon etc. though I wasn't actually into reading much back then growing up at *Inukan House* in Ibadan, Nigeria.

When I read this book, it was like a message to me and the people who are close to me on how to reshape my financial lifestyle. Though, the *Savings* chapter is my favourite part of the book but Niyi touched some other areas that I am going to adopt to my lifestyle and will surely advice people around me to do the same.

This is a must-read book; simple and educative which anyone who has the privilege should to go and grab fast - for their family's financial future.

Colin Adeoshun-Peters
CEO, Risocrat Int'l (Nig) Ltd, Lagos, Nigeria

Over the years I have known Niyi to be very principled in his approach, this book is no different. 1 love the humour and simplicity in which it is written; quite straightforward and down to earth. It covers key areas to set anyone on the right path to a sound financial future, things like diligence with our work, the discipline of saving & giving, investments, the dangers of gambling and much more.

In my opinion it is a must read for parents to educate their children early in life to avoid the pitfalls and the excesses regarding money setting them on the right path financially, this book has set the pace for financial wisdom.

I would advise that our youth grab a hold of it, read it and begin applying the wealth of the wisdom that is on the inside. As it is often said the words of our elders are indeed words of wisdom, thank God for the life of our Papa Adeoshun and the legacy he left behind for us to glean through this book.

Happy reading. God bless.

Pastor Toyin Jama
President, Sisters' Fellowship, NLBC, London UK

I am so honoured to be given the privilege to review this book by Niyi Adeoshun, who incidentally is my younger brother. Apart from the lessons taught, it brings back the exciting memories of our growing years and the immense impact of our father's mentoring on all of us.

The style of presentation of the lessons makes the book educative and interesting to read. In fact, readers are in for thrilling moments because the book is spiced with lots of true life stories and dialogues which make reading pleasurable. Niyi went a step further by including some quotes and Bible verses. I am particularly thrilled by this because it attests to the fact that God is the Author and Sustainer of wealth.

I will like to emphasize that beyond reading this book, readers should try to put the lessons therein into actions because it is only through your action that you can fully benefit and maximize your gains which will invariably result from reading this book, which is a road map to wealth creation. I therefore recommend without reservation *"**Financial Legacy**: 8 Lessons My Father Taught me about Money"*, with which you will be empowered and attain financial success far beyond what you ever thought or imagined to be possible.

Mrs. Olabisi Arinola Olaniran (Nee Adeoshun)
Pastor, Life Assembly, Ibadan
Principal, Celestial Church of Christ High
School, Ibadan. Nigeria.

Dedication

To

My father,
Late Pa Peter Ijaola Adeoshun (Inukan),
who in his own loving way has been a profound
influence on my life through his non-
compromising inner-conviction and personal
ethics.

and

My sons
Vincent, Christopher and **David**
to whom I have the opportunity of passing my
financial legacy.

Acknowledgement

I wrote this book alone (mostly) because I had to dig deep into my memory banks for many weeks trying hard to accurately recall certain evergreen but life-changing events in my past. Through it all, my wonderful wife, Joyce, and our boys supported me enormously; for which I am very grateful.

I would like to give a special thanks to my sister, Mrs. Bolanle Aderogba, for acting as my 'sounding-board' when I needed to verify some aspects of our younger days.

I would like to thank Efua Ochu, my ever-faithful proof-reader, for helping me to polish the book to its current state.

My appreciation goes to businesswoman Kemi Abe – my niece and my father's first grandchild, for sparing the time to write the foreword. To the reviewers of the book, Pastor Toyin Jama, Chinedu Onyemobi, Colin Peters-Adeoshun and Mrs Bisi Olaniran, I say "thank you" from the bottom of my heart.

Most of all I want to thank the Almighty God for the gifts of memories (for looking back into yesteryears) and imagination (for looking forward to years to come). I used both extensively for this book to be completed and to Him be all the glory forever.

Foreword

In today's world, there is a growing realization that financial intelligence, as distinct from formal education or vocational skills, is not only desirable but critical to sustainable prosperity and true financial freedom. Many highly educated people are grossly deficient with regard to wealth creation in a sustainable way; much less leave an inheritance for their children.

This book, FINANCIAL LEGACY, is a timely attempt by the author to fill this gap by sharing with us certain principles of financial intelligence and their practical applications as learnt from his own father, who apparently modelled those principles during his lifetime with impressive and lasting results.

The author (my uncle) uses as a springboard the words of Don Patterson that, "An inheritance is what you leave FOR someone, while a legacy is what you leave IN someone". In his treatment of the subject of Financial Legacy, the author comes across clearly as one in whom his father has truly left a priceless legacy – one that is worth sharing with the whole world.

Niyi Adeoshun, in this simple, readable and yet profound work, has been able to share from his personal experiences, exposing readers to the power of influential parenting, having imbibed informally from his father's life some timeless lessons in money management and prudent investment, among others.

I do recall, though vaguely, the zeal with which my grandfather (the author's father) studied the newspapers; looking out daily for which stocks were doing well. It seemed so meaningless at the time, until I had the opportunity to work in a stock broking firm decades after. It was then that I realized what must have informed my grandfather's passion for newspapers. He did earn more of my respect from then on.

From the lessons highlighted in this piece, it is clear that the book is all-encompassing and its message timeless. The eight lessons, briefly captured, include: *the need for deliberate decision-making coupled with focus; pursuing one's passion; purposeful saving and avoidance of debt; protection from financial disaster; understanding risks and rewards; non-*

dependence on luck; the value of destiny helpers as well as generosity as a lifestyle.

While commending the unique style and efforts of the author, I strongly recommend this book to fathers (and mothers alike), young adults and even children not just because of my historical link to the author and his father, but because I am convinced it will make valuable reading to all. This is a chronicle of a worthy legacy – one that I am proud to be a part of.

Olukemi Abe (Mrs)
CEO, Marvel Place, Lagos, Nigeria

Contents

Introduction

A little while ago, one of my clients (now a good friend) informed me that she wanted to do something special in memory of her grandfather. She asked me to build a website in his honour (showing his family tree, etc.) in time for the 25th anniversary of his death. She said due to the fact that she lost her father at a very young age, her grandfather was the main father figure that she had during her formative years.

This got me thinking about the influence of fathers on their children, especially the influence of my father on my siblings and me. We turned out alright; so our father must have done a good job.

I have always viewed myself as being blessed in many ways in my life. One of those ways was having my father present while I was growing up. I had many friends who would have given anything to have the love, care and guidance that I got from my father.

Many people are of the opinion that leaving an inheritance like money, properties, stocks and shares, etc., for their children will make their lives better. Don't get me wrong; if you have the means to do that, please do it – it will make a huge difference to your dependants. For those who cannot do this, take heart. Rich or poor, every parent has the opportunity of passing down something better and much more advantageous than an inheritance – and that is a **legacy**.

Don Patterson said, *"An inheritance is what you leave FOR someone; a legacy is what you leave IN someone".*

I didn't have a Rich Dad or Poor Dad; I had an upper-middle-class Dad who was wise enough to know that if you cultivate the habits of the rich, you will eventually become rich. Not only that, he also passed those habits to us - his children.

I can say my sensitivity to good management of money came from my father as a legacy to me. It is now up to me to pass on to my children whatever I think they may need in the years to come.

What have your parents taught you about money that is influencing your financial life today?

A child can be hurt in a thousand different ways from the lessons they are taught and from the lessons that no one taught him or her.

Truth be told, the financial situations faced by our parents were quite different from ours these days, which will not be the same as the ones our children will face in the years to come. The principles of staying on top of your finances, however, are the same from generation to generation.

Those evergreen principles are what I intend to share with you in this book. It is about the money lessons that I learnt from my father.

My hope is that this book will spur you on to begin building a good Financial Legacy into your loved ones.

To Your Success,

Niyi Adeoshun
Money Management Coach

Chapter 1

My First Financial Lesson

I remember as if it were yesterday, on my 13th birthday, my father beckoned to me after the family morning devotion. He said he wanted to show me something.

As I followed him out to the balcony, I started thinking, "*This has got to be good. I must be getting a very special present this year*".

When we got there, he asked me to wait, and he didn't say anything for about two minutes. He just kept looking out for something or someone - My birthday present? Maybe...

"Watch this", my father said, and like clockwork, the newspaper vendor that served our street came round the corner. When he got to our house, he exchanged pleasantries with my father, delivered the newspapers and just left —

without bringing out a special "something" from a hidden pocket for me!

After the man had gone, my father sat me down and gave me a glimpse of what my life could be like in any circumstance – depending on the decisions I was willing to make.

He told me that the vendor, that just left, had fallen on hard times. As just a teenager, he lost his father and had to start working early in life to be able to support his mother and sisters. He held several jobs at the same time, including the newspaper vendor 'gig'.

While I was wondering what all that had to do with me - on my birthday, my father asked me an unexpected question, "If you find yourself in such a situation, what would you do?"

That wasn't the kind of question I liked answering, but I answered him anyway. I said "I too would go out and work" – even though I had never done a day's paid work in my life!

He then asked me, "Then what?"

I looked at him blankly and answered, "I don't know. I will just w-w-work".

My First Financial Lesson

My father looked at me straight in the eyes and said, "If you only want to work for survival, you might as well start selling newspapers now, but if not, you must have a really good reason why you will be working and what you want to do with the money you will make."

He then went on to give me a modern-day run-through of the legendary *"The Richest Man in Babylon"* in only 10 minutes. He talked to me about doing well in school, graduating, working, saving and spending money, how to enjoy life within reason, etc.

When he finally stopped, I asked him "How do I do all that?"

He replied, "I don't expect you to understand everything now, but one day you will. You just need to make up your mind, and you can be *anything* you want to be; do *anything* you want to do, and have *anything* you want to have. How you will accomplish that is another matter."

My father rounded up our time together that early morning by telling me a story, which, incidentally, our Principal in high school repeated to us a few months later.

The story went like this:

> *There was once, in a village, a wise old man famous for being able to tell what other people were thinking.*
>
> *One of the young men in the village decided one day to prove that the wise man was not as wise as everyone thought he was.*
>
> *With a bird in his hand, he approached the old man, showed him the beak of the tiny bird sticking out from his fist, and said, "Old man, tell me: is this bird dead or alive?" The old man looked at him and replied calmly, "The answer to that question lies totally in YOUR hands."*
>
> *The wise old man went on by saying, "If I say the bird is dead, you will release your grip and allow the bird to fly away. If I say the bird is alive, you could squeeze it so tight that it would immediately die. **So all in all, it is in YOUR hands**".*

I can't even remember what present I got for my 13th birthday, but I can never forget my first financial lesson

So what was my first (official) financial lesson?

Decision.

My father wanted me to decide what I desired in life from an early age so I could go all out and get it. It is like *beginning with the end in mind.*

Daniel Boone said, *"Having an exciting destination is like setting a needle in your compass. From then on, the compass knows only one point - its ideal. And it will faithfully guide you there through the darkest nights and the fiercest storms"*

You see, it is a well-established fact that successful people make plans about their lives' directions early and then spend the rest of their lives carrying out those plans. On the other hand, there are also many people with no focus; jumping *from pillar to post;* being too busy *with* life to make any progress *in* it; they have activity but without productivity; marching all day long on a single spot and going nowhere.

If you want to be successful, you need to decide what you want to be or have and focus on it with all your daily activities.

Many decisions we make will cause dramatic changes in our minds in an instant; the physical manifestation may take some time to come. It does not matter if we are starting a new project, giving up a habit, or making some other changes in our lives which will affect us for years to come, but we will experience the consequences of our decisions eventually.

I would like to add here that a decision alone without action is worthless, and action taken without first making a firm decision can end up being a nightmare for you. You must work on your decision to acquire your desire.

If your lack of making firm decisions has cost you dearly in your life, would you want your children to go through the same thing? I suppose not.

If that is the case, help them early in life to learn the power of focus, so that when they eventually decide their paths in life, reaching their goals will not be too difficult.

Chapter 2

Do What You Love

My father owned and operated a Medicine Store in Ibadan, Nigeria, for several decades. It was a business he started from nothing, built up and operated until he retired. As with any parent, he desired to have one of his children succeed him in this business; to carry on his legacy, so to speak. As an innocent child, I unwittingly offered myself for that *prestigious* position. It happened like this...

Together with my siblings, I used to visit my father at his Store sometimes during school holidays, and on many occasions, we would all go back home together with him. Along the route back to our house, we used to drive past two Chemists called 'Rab & Lali Chemists' and 'Toye Chemist'; I remember announcing to (and later reminding) everyone in the car that when

I grew up, I would own a Chemist and call my business **"Niyi Chemist"**.

That was a joy for my father. To spur me on even more, he would proudly tell anyone who would listen that I was going to study Pharmacy at the university – even though I was still in elementary school!

By the time I was halfway through high school, however, any mention of Pharmacy was becoming rather uncomfortable for me because everything electronic had become my passion. Physics and mathematics were my best subjects in school. Also, I had gradually developed a dislike for Biology (a necessary subject for the study of Pharmacy) and my overly strict Biology teacher did not help matters as far as I was concerned.

When I made engineering my first-choice course for university, my father was a bit disappointed – even though he didn't verbalise it. He, however, told me that he would rather have me study a course that I liked and would enjoy working at than do anything else. This was a relief for me as I had been apprehensive about telling him that Pharmacy was not the way for me. My father still got his wish; because one of my junior brothers loved and excelled in chemistry and is now an accomplished Pharmacist.

When I graduated with an honours degree in Electrical & Electronics Engineering, my father and I both got something precious out of it. He got his first engineer in the family, and I got to follow my passion. I'd say that's a 'Win-Win' situation if you ask me.

Keep Learning

After education come, the opportunities to put what you've learnt into fruitful practice. Classroom education is one thing; it gives you a 'leg-up' into your career choice. Education for developing that career is another, and this one will not be thrust on you. You have to go after it.

My father told me after graduation to **never stop learning**. The fact that you have graduated does not mean that your education has come to an end. To become an expert in your field, you must keep on learning more in your chosen profession.

My father didn't have the opportunities that I had in education. In fact, he was self-taught; he sat for his examinations through Correspondence Courses with colleges in the UK. Using the same process, he learnt to speak several languages in addition. He had a strong desire to be educated, so when people around him stopped learning, he followed his dreams. His education, though limited, still afforded him better choices in life than many of his contemporaries. So I reckon he knew what he was talking about when he told me not to stop learning.

From statistics, it has been deduced that the average man or woman reads about one book every year. If YOU, as an individual, spend about 30 to 60 minutes a day reading up on any subject or field of study, you will be reading an average of at least 1 book a month. So in 5 years' time, when the average person would have read 5 books – if any at all, you would have read 60 books!! Tell me, who would have more information or expertise then?

If you want to get better at what you do, then continue to read (and learn) and also teach your offspring to develop this same habit.

Be Productive

One of the responsibilities of fathers is to teach their children how to be productive on their own.

To be a productive person (and on a daily basis), you will be working your mind, working your body or both. A manual worker has to work his body all day long, while an administrative officer mostly works his brain – hopefully. Your education (and profession) will decide which one you use more and how much you are paid for it. In both cases, you have to work in order to produce.

Contrary to what many people believe, work is not a necessary evil but a blessing. Imagine what will happen to us all if we just lounge around all day doing nothing, we will waste away - literally. Have you also noticed that you enjoy (and treat well) something that you have worked for?

Don't just work, be productive, **do what you love** and more importantly, **love what you do**. If you don't, the grind of '9-5' (or whatever periods you work) will take its toll on you, and it will reveal itself in your health and your emotions.

You may not be where you hope to be yet, but try and enjoy where you are now; there is reward in the education you will receive there.

If you can work hard at what you love, your vocation will eventually become your vacation, as you will enjoy it so much.

Being Independent

I know my father had several jobs earlier in his working life. One of them was being a Shopkeeper, and according to him, he got some of his best education in salesmanship there.

My father was hardworking and enterprising but he deduced that if he was going to be as rich as he wanted, he had to establish his own business. Going against the grain of working for someone else took a lot of courage on his part, but he did it anyway. He said he wanted to control his own destiny by grabbing the opportunities presented to him with both hands.

Does everybody have to establish his or her own enterprise? Not necessarily, but you need to know that whatever your job is, you, as an individual, must be doing something daily to build your own dreams instead of just building someone else's. Everybody has a product or service he or she can offer for profit, and that includes you.

Some people have the illusion of thinking their jobs are 'secure'. My father told me once that **"If you don't own it, you can't control it."** If you are just *adequate* for your job, you are dispensable. You can be replaced at any time with another *adequate* person; your position can be deemed redundant, and your duties distributed among other employees. What will you do then?

What do you desire to be, to do or to have? Work towards what those desires are. Your desires should produce some motivation in you; motivation usually produces discipline; discipline produces actions; consistent, productive actions will eventually result in your desires becoming realities.

Let's say you have a 'business' – the product or service that you can make money from (full-time or part-time); for it to grow, you must be able to sell.

Sell?
Yes, **sell**.

Everyone sells something every day. When you attend an interview, you are trying to sell yourself, i.e. your qualifications, skills and abilities. Even if you're a published author like me, you have to be able to sell. They don't usually give prizes for being a best-writing author but for being a best-selling author!

You may say, "What if I really don't know how to sell anything?" In that case, get partners who can. That would be my simple answer for now. We will deal with this aspect of business in a later chapter.

All I'm trying to say here is that whatever you do, do something daily to put yourself in a position to become financially independent.

Let Integrity Rule Your Actions

In the process of trying to climb up your career ladder or in building your business, you may be presented with 'opportunities' to take shortcuts that you know are not right. Be careful and do what is right.

Do What You Love

Warren Buffett said, *"It takes 20 years to build a reputation but five minutes to ruin it. If you think about that, you'll do things differently."* You cannot put any kind of gains above your integrity; it's just not worth it.

To be a person of integrity means people can count on or depend upon you. It means your word is your bond; if you say that you are going to provide a service or product for a certain amount of money, then you do it. You are looking out for the good of both your customers, as well as yourself.

In business, as in life, your reputation will always precede you! These days, word (good or bad; mostly bad) spreads quite rapidly on the internet. Make it easy for your loved ones to defend you. The bible says in Proverbs 20:7, **"A righteous man who walks in his integrity; How blessed are his sons after him."**

Don't participate in businesses that involve any form of dishonesty, lying or cheating on taxes. Edwin Louis Cole said, *"Half-truth is a whole lie."*

A liar must have a very good memory, as he has to cover his tracks with more lies, and thus he has no room in his brain to do better and useful things. By the way, your partners in crime will have no qualms about cheating you too!

Who do you think you are really cheating when you lie and steal to get money that you can't keep or enjoy when nobody wants to do business with you anymore?

Keep your word; deal with people honestly; allow nothing but the truth to be found in you. Your integrity (coupled with excellent product and service) will make people want to do business with you more and more, and thus you will make more money. If, on the other hand, people don't trust you and the news goes round...., God help you and your business.

There is nothing that cannot be repaired. If your integrity is already in tatters, stop doing the old dishonest stuff and begin re-building the trust again; no matter how long it takes.

Watch out!! There are people with no morals who are quite happy to make money by ripping you off and scamming you of your hard-earned money! If a deal is too good to be true, it probably is. If in doubt, don't do it!

My father used to say that **"it is better to get rich in steady trickles than to lose all you have because you are seeking a glut."** Fraudsters are counting on your inclination to greed. Don't be greedy, and you will save yourself a whole lot of headaches.

Teach your children about the gift, adventure and rewards of work. Let them know that integrity should be their watchword in everything and the reasons why.

Chapter 3

Save Purposefully and Avoid Debt like a Plague

You may be wondering why I put savings and avoidance of debt in the same chapter since they don't go together. Well, in life, you cannot be digging a hole and be getting out of it at the same time. It is equally foolish to think you can be saving money while you are getting deeper into debt at the same time. You will be pulled in one direction or the other at any one time.

I will tell you about my lesson on savings first.

Saving with Purpose

A Japanese proverb says, "*Getting money is like digging with a nail; spending it is like water soaking into the sand*". This shows, as we all know, that it is easier and more fun to spend money than to acquire it.

My father hated stupidity, especially when it had to do with money. (Actually, most things in life has to do with money, one way or the other.) He also could not stand waste of any kind; maybe due to his upbringing in a poor family.

I must confess that I demonstrated a fair bit of financial stupidity as a child – not from lack of money but from having a bit too much of it for my intelligence.

With the number of uncles and aunties that I had on both of my parents' sides, it was just impossible for me not to have cash gifts from them time and again. My 'wisdom' back then did not exceed keeping the money for a while until it was time to blow the **whole** amount on the next bright, shiny thing that came along.

My parents encouraged me to open an account with the Federal Savings Bank in my first year in high school. It was actually a Post Office account which you could open with only 10pence – back then in the mid-70s. The 'bank' was established to encourage people to save more. My father's point was to decrease the ease of access that I had to my money, and that I would have time to think before withdrawing money and spending it all.

It worked. Seeing my money increase every time my 'passbook' was updated created an unexplainable excitement in me. For those who don't know what 'passbooks' are: they served (in the pre-digital age) as your copy of the records of deposit and withdrawals - written by hand and later with printers.

Saving money is an important habit parents should teach their children. Mind you, it is not a natural habit, just as brushing our teeth is not a natural habit either. They both have to be learned and done.

One way to do this is to open a savings account in the child's name. If parents have the expertise, older children can be taught about other types of savings and investments, which I will go into later in this book.

Your teenagers can be taught the benefits of compounding interest and learn to set aside money for the emergencies that occur in everyone's life.

Financial Legacy

Saving money is good, but don't overdo it.

The first time I made a withdrawal from my savings account, I bought a wristwatch – my very first one. After that, I began saving every penny I could lay my hands on. I wanted to buy bigger and better things.

One day, my father asked me what I was saving for.
I replied to him, saying "Nothing in particular, but when I see it I will know it."

"So in the meantime, the money keeps growing in your account. Right?" he asked again.

"Yes. That's the point," I replied with pride.

"Have you thought of giving part of it away?" my father asked – off the subject, I might add.

"Give?" I asked, wondering what he was getting at.

"Yes. Give." He confirmed.

My father then asked me, "Do you know that there's just a thin line between saving and hoarding?" Without waiting for me to answer, he explained saying, "When you save money, there is normally a specific purpose in mind. It may be either a short-term or a long-term purpose. Hoarding, on the other hand, is putting money aside without establishing any specific goal or use for that money. You just DON'T want anyone's hands on it"

The amount I had at the bank at the time of this discussion above was less than $100 (100 naira at that time), but that did not stop greed from creeping in. Greed does not come into play because of the amount you possess, it is a matter of the heart.

Allow me to clarify here that even though an emergency fund is not for a 'specific purpose', **but it has a limit,** which is usually about 3 to 6 months' value of your living expenses. (I explained this more in my book "*Milestones of Financial Freedom*"). Any excess after that should be used for other purposes like investing, children's university funds, paying off the mortgage, increased charitable giving, etc.

It is not only in saving money that hoarding rears its head; for other *stuff,* we sometimes say, "I don't want to lose this because I may need it later." We end up moving unneeded and unused *stuff*from house to house instead of giving them away. Has this happened to you before?

We will deal more with *Giving* in a later chapter.

Avoiding Financial Black Holes

When people are not saving, they are spending, and sometimes the spending can turn into overspending. If the overspending is not brought under control in time, debt and its problems may set in.

From my childhood, I had realised that my father hated debt or anything that looked like it. Don't even talk to him about borrowing anything from a friend – no matter how friendly you are with that person. (Books needed for a short period of time were okay.) If you lend out an item and your friend doesn't return it, my father would tell you to choose between your friendship and that item because you will lose one or both of them soon.

I didn't understand why until I began my career and started to acquire things that my heart desired – without having the funds to get them. I have learnt since then that debt changes relationships. For example, you may have been a model customer to your bank for a long time, but once you borrow from them, you become a *slave* to them because you are no longer working for yourself alone. You now work with the repayment of your debt constantly on your mind.

I can never forget my father telling me many times that *"assumption is the lowest form of knowledge"*. People assume a lot of things when it comes to finances, especially debt. They assume that things will always be the same; that they will still be in good health and in employment; that the economy will be the same or even better, etc. Things can change when you least expect them and thus put you in a financial bind. This is the risk that all debts carry.

Borrowing for short-term happiness can bring long-term misery.

I hate (with a passion) those adverts suggesting that you should borrow money for the holiday of a lifetime, or a brand spanking new TV, etc. The fact that credit is easily accessible for you and someone told you that *"you are credit-worthy"* does not mean that you should go ahead and borrow money!

As a rule, you should only really borrow for items that appreciate in value (such as a property); even with those, you should pay a large deposit to begin with. You should not borrow money to buy things just because you **want** them– even if you think you can make the monthly payments now.

Use the desire or goal of going on the holiday or of owning that new electronic gadget as the motivation you need to save the money for it first.

My parents never had credit cards partly because they never had access to such items during their working lives. Even if they did, I am absolutely sure they would not get one. *The short-term happiness you get from using borrowed money cannot be compared to the long-term misery that debt brings.*

Tackle the problem

Life happens, and things usually don't go according to plan when you have a debt hanging around your neck. If things go wrong, then it is essential that you confront the problem immediately.

Contact anybody you owe money to and make them aware of your financial difficulties. Tell them the truth; the first stage of sorting things out is accepting that there is a problem.

I saw my father deal with the problems of some relatives who fell on hard times and came to him for advice. One of the first things he did was to establish the position where the person could be best helped.

He would ask questions such as:
- "Do you owe this money?"
- "Are you behind in your payments?"
- "Does this mean you are not keeping your end of the contract?"
- "What do we do now?"

There is no apportioning of blame or finding excuses at this stage; just accept your responsibility, and the debt problem can be tackled better. My father would say to them that the exercise was to put them in a favourable position with the Lenders under their current circumstances.

Lenders will often be more understanding than you think, especially when they don't have to chase you for months before you get in touch with them.

Even if you don't have money troubles and can make your monthly payments, you still need to do all you can to get out of debt.

Please note that you have to hatefully despise debt to get out of it. Don't treat any debt like a pet that you just need to keep feeding for a long time to come. Get rid of it as quickly as you can!

Change the story

Many people grew up in families that had everything but owned nothing; their 'possessions' had been acquired on credit. Being in debt was a way of life growing up, so when they became adults, they saw no reason to even try to be out of debt, and so the story continues to the next generation.

As we mature, we usually incorporate many of our parents' and society's attitudes about money into our lives. These include many of the myths about money floating around, such as: money is the root of all evil; if I had enough money, I would be happy, etc.

But wait, won't it be better if your children could control their finances instead of debt controlling them?

To change your family tree financially, your children should not make the same mistakes you made with money and it is your duty to set them a better example than the ones they are witnessing all around the country. So get your acts together and allow your children to see a financially new you – someone they can emulate.

Chapter 4

Prepare for the Unexpected

I have seen many nasty injuries on the football field in every league; bones being broken; legs hanging at awkward angles after an ill-timed or vicious tackle. The injured players may be out of action for many months, even up to two years, but most of them get back on the field and begin playing football again — just like before.

How could they do that?

Determination!
The unreserved resolution to get back on their feet!!

Of course, these players have the backing of good medical personnel. That, some money, and their never-give-up attitudes are their protection from professional disaster.

Do you know that many individuals and businesses are operating on the edge of disaster every day? What I mean is that just ONE mishap, accident or loss can spell financial troubles or even bankruptcy for individuals or businesses.

How do you protect yourself from financial disaster? ...**By being properly insured.**

My belief in carrying adequate insurance for financial survival started with an incident at my father's business many years ago.

My father was in partnership for many decades with a Scottish man called George Lockhart, and part of his business was ordering medicine from the UK (through George Lockhart Ltd) to be distributed through many outlets in several regions of Nigeria and some other West African countries.

The distribution was usually done by road, with company trucks.

On one of those trips, one truck carrying newly-approved medicine (very expensive cargo!) had an accident. Everything was lost, the truck was written off; even my father's relation, who travelled on the truck, lost a hand. Apart from the lengthy hospital stay, the personnel were okay, but the merchandise was gone.

There was a lot riding on that particular trip because of its special cargo; so when the accident happened, the business was as good as gone – except for the fact that there was adequate insurance on the personnel, the cargo and the truck!

Nobody, that I know, enjoys paying insurance premiums, but when the unforeseen happens, we are usually glad we made those payments.

In the previous chapter, I mentioned having an emergency fund which should take care of any unexpected expenses (from a blocked sink to busted tyres) that may arise in any month. There are, however, things that come up that are bigger than your income or Emergency Fund. This is where insurance comes in.

Having adequate insurance on things such as vehicles, income, health, life etc., does not stop the 'bad' event from occurring, but it helps you avert financial disaster by transferring the risk of replacing what you have lost to someone else, i.e. the insurance companies.

Practice putting yourself in a position which will allow you to 'bounce back' after an unfortunate event in life. Insurance can help you turn a setback into a stepping-stone for a new 'comeback'.

Don't just practice having good financial protection; teach your children the same. This is a good legacy to leave.

Chapter 5

Understanding Risks and Rewards

"I like Michael Jackson, but I still like Coke better than Pepsi". This was my father's comment while we were watching one of those 'hair-burning, scalp-frying' Pepsi adverts that MJ did in the 80s.

We all looked at my father, wondering what he was talking about, before one of my sisters asked the question that was on all our minds, "You don't even like soft drinks, how can you say you love Pepsi or Coke?

My father used that as an opportunity to inform us of the fact that he had shares in the Coca-Cola Bottling Company. So, as long as the company was doing well and making profits, he was sure his money there will continue to make him more money.

Financial Legacy

At that point in time I knew very little about what investing was but I gathered that it was something you do on top of your savings and mostly after paying off debt.

As anyone should know, there is no amount of money you can save from your income that would be enough for you to live on at retirement age, for most people at least. What do you do? Invest for the future, of course.

To begin with, you must realise that the money you invest must be left untouched for at least 5 years or better still, until you retire. That is the reason why you should not begin putting money away while you're still struggling with debt, because you cannot afford to lose *that* money.

Investigate Before You Invest

On the subject of 'losing money', many people refuse to invest (especially in the stock market) because of the 'risk' it carries. Warren Buffett, the world-renowned Investor, billionaire, and philanthropist, said, *"Risk comes from not knowing what you're doing."*

If you invest in things that you don't understand, then you are just saying that by some luck you will *profit* from the stock market. That's not the right way to invest – you might as well be gambling, and I do not advise that.

When I was in primary school, I used to get injured a lot while playing sports, so I found it easier to just stay out of the way of any contact sport for fear of injuries (and read novels instead). I have learned a lot since those days.

"Courage isn't absence of fear, it is the awareness that something else is important"
- Stephen R. Covey

It has been said that **winners are not afraid to lose, because failure is a part of the process of success.** People who are afraid to fail lose out on the opportunity to succeed.

Everything you want to accomplish has its risks and rewards – just like the two sides of a coin. For example, in the purchase of a house, on one hand, it may seem to look like you're buying an asset as it will appreciate but on the other hand, it might be a liability because of the additional expenses, such as upkeep and insurance and taxes, it would incur. You need to always weigh your options; the risks, the rewards and then put your decisions into action.

Enterprise before Pleasure

The Bible says in Proverbs 24:27, *"Prepare your work without, and make it fit for yourself in the field; and afterwards build your house."* What this means can simply be put as 'enterprise before pleasure'.

Do what you must - to put into motion what will feed you, before you start eating from it. Build businesses first to have multiple sources of income, then you can relax in pleasure later on.

We live in a world where everyone wants to *plant* today and *reap the harvest* tomorrow, but hard work and patience must come before good results. You must 'risk' a little time in the present to get the 'reward' in the future.

The game **Monopoly** is one of the most popular proprietary board games in the world. It combines fast-paced action with intense business dealings where players compete to buy properties and build houses & hotels on vacant lots. Every single game is different and involves intense wheeling and dealing among the players.

One of the strategies to win the game is to buy as many properties as possible **in the beginning**. The more property you have, the higher your potential to collect rent, and the more rent you collect, the more money you get and the sooner you can win the game.

Robert Kiyosaki, author of the bestseller, "**Rich Dad Poor Dad**", said in the book that acquiring 4 green houses and 1 red hotel wins the game of Monopoly. Try it and find out for yourself.

My father told me something just before I left home 'to find my path in life'; he said, "**Don't just look for a job, open your eyes to other opportunities. You cannot get rich with just a job alone because the *security* you seek in some jobs may keep you from being what you are supposed to be in life.**"

I guess he knew I had a better chance of seeing my dreams come true if I broke free from the herd mentality of not investing my time, money, or energy very well.

People are afraid of taking risks, so they miss out on the rewards. Actually, a loser is someone who is afraid of losing. Don't let the fear of losing keep you from winning.

Children can begin to learn some principles of financial management if parents are willing to invest the time it takes to teach them.

Every one of us is predominantly a spender, a saver or a giver. Each of these traits has its risks and rewards. One way parents can teach their children is to allow them to acquire a little money to *work* with. This might be through a small allowance or perhaps payment for certain tasks they can do around the house.

When children receive money, help them learn how to manage it. They should learn to save, spend and give. They should learn not to be afraid of stepping out and doing something with their money which will bring in *more* money.

If you are running scared of taking calculated risks and losing out on financial rewards, what do you think your children are learning from that? What legacy of risks and rewards are you leaving them?

Chapter 6

Don't Depend on Luck

My family enjoyed watching football for the sake of the game, but there are other people who like football more for the results than the game itself.

My earliest recollection of any form of gambling must be the 'Pools' in the 70s – I think they called it *"Face-To-Face"* pools. In those days, anytime I went to the barbershop, there were always discussions about which English or Scottish teams would win at the weekend or how many 'draws' they (the punters) would guess correctly that time.

(My father always said it was ridiculous for someone living in Nigeria to be throwing his hard-earned money at the outcome of some football matches being played in another country thousands of miles away!)

These punters would gather around the radio just about the time the British league matches were being completed. As the final results were announced, the men would, one after the other, begin ripping up their betting slip for the week – they had lost again.

The fact that these men (usually) were losing only small amounts of money every week, combined with some sporadic wins, did not wake them to the realisation that the organisers of the Pools were the real winners.

If by some *chance* the punters won at all, they would *blow* the winnings on alcohol without thinking of the amount they had lost in the months or years gone by. In my opinion, depending on luck seemed to relieve people of their senses in a way.

That was over forty years ago. Things have not changed, in real terms, since those days. Nowadays, pool agents operate betting shops with multiple TV screens so punters can watch their money go down the drain, so to speak. They no longer just bet on football but on all sports in addition to dog and horse racing. You can even bet on how long a politician will stay in office before being kicked out for one offence or the other!

My father taught me (and my siblings) not to depend on luck, gamble or play the lottery. His reasoning always started with "***A bird in hand is better than two in the bush***". He would tell us to stay in control of our money and that by throwing it at a 'lucky' scheme, it is as good as gone forever.

Millions of people are spending at least £1 or $1 regularly each week on the lottery with the hope of, one day, winning millions of dollars. Even though the majority would never win, they continue to play. Why?

Gambling is false logic and arrogance rolled into one senseless action.

The problem with gambling is the arrogance that says you are going to win when nobody else does. This is the core thinking behind gambling.

By the way, gambling is not entertainment. Some gambling organisations have tried to explain gambling away as harmless 'entertainment'. Not on your life. There is nothing entertaining in losing money. Find other ways to entertain yourself that will not cause you to lose your spouse and your house.

You should also stop saying things like "I wish I could just be lucky". This shouldn't even be in your vocabulary. Instead of wishing, why not "**just do it**" like NIKE™ says? Do something about what you are wishing for; who knows, you might just get it.

Alexander Woollcott said, *"Many of us spend half of our time wishing for things we could have if we didn't spend half our time wishing."*

Am I inferring from the above quotation that gamblers are lazy? Not necessarily. In fact, people think that laziness is the opposite of hard work. No, it is not. The Bible says in Proverbs 21:5 that *"The plans of the diligent lead surely to plenty, but those of everyone who is hasty, surely to poverty."*

HASTE is the opposite of hard work. Profiting from hard work takes time, but gambling in any form is done with the hope of getting a lot with no effort *and* in no time.

The Bible says in Proverbs 12:11 that *"He who works his land will have abundant food, but he who chases fantasies lacks judgment."* (NIV)

All forms of gambling are like chasing fantasy. You never catch it.

If you are involved in gambling, what do you think your children will learn from your actions?

The legacy of hard work never ends with the original worker; if done well, your children and grandchildren can benefit from it.

Chapter 7

You Can't Do Everything by Yourself

I have included this chapter because most of the things you will accomplish in life will involve the input of other people. As it is said, *"no man is an island"*.

My Pastor, Richard Jama, once said that *"All destinies are interconnected and no destiny is fulfilled in isolation."* How you will succeed in life is usually linked in some way to how you can help others to succeed. Always think 'Win-Win'.

Who are those around you that are influencing you, growing with you or diminishing your efforts?

I worked for a company in Surrey, UK that was started by three partners. One was in charge of the design of their main product –

software, one was in charge of marketing, and the third partner was in charge of administration. Each partner was the best at what he did, and by putting his best into his area of strength, each helped grow the business in his own way. This system was followed until they sold the business for huge profits years later.

Do what you are best at and allow others to help you do the things that they are best at. For you to succeed, you must learn to allow the strength of others to lift you.

In the primary school that I attended, Baptist Day School, we were allowed to come to school in ordinary clothes on our birthdays instead of the school uniform. The celebrant will usually bring cookies and sweets to be distributed amongst his or her classmates. This practice allowed some of us to have two parties – one in school and the other at home.

I learnt a powerful lesson on the day I turned 10 years old that I will never forget. When it was time for the stuff I brought to be distributed, the Teacher asked how it should be done. I described to her how I *thought* it should be done.

The teacher then said, "if you so know how to do it, I think you should do it yourself". With that, she went behind her desk and sat down. She said nothing about the goodies till the end of the school day. I cried all the way home and told my parents that the teacher hated me.

On hearing what *actually* happened, my parents informed me that I had a good teacher. They said what the woman was trying to teach me was the importance of partnership; that I didn't know everything; that I had to learn to let people use their strengths to lift me up.

My goodies were distributed the following day, just like the teacher used to do, but after I had learnt my lesson.

Many people, out of fear or pride, would never let their plans be known to those who could have helped bring them to fruition.

Apart from George Lockhart, my father's business partner in the United Kingdom, my father had two other partners who, though they had their own businesses, had influence in what businesses he succeeded in, just as he did in theirs.

They had the habit of bouncing ideas off one another, weighing the pros and cons before committing funds to those ideas. These partnerships worked for all of them, even after their working days.

I must not fail to mention that the best partner you can have is your spouse. If you have one, be happy. He or she will not only be your support emotionally but will be your 'sound of reason' as well. Women perform this role very well – at least my wife does.

Men, do not allow pride to debar you from benefiting from the intuitive mind that God has given your wives. The two of you may not think alike, but you must learn to think together. Your logic and her intuition will make you a powerful force.

Young men and women, you can benefit from the wisdom and experience of a Mentor. Find one, be humble, be receptive, be ready to learn and to put what you have learnt into practice.

Chapter 8

Be Generous

I have seen greedy poor people in my life, just as I have seen greedy rich people. Greed has little to do with how much you possess; it is a condition of the heart.

How then does one guard against greed?

By being generous, not out of guilt or emotional manipulation, but from the goodness of your heart.

When you give something from your heart without expecting anything in return, you release a powerful force that will trigger your good deed to "bounce" back to you in amazing and sometimes unusual ways.

My father was a very generous person; not only to his extended family but many other people as well. Sometimes he would tell us why he did some generous thing; other times his only explanation would be "**It just felt like a good thing to do**".

As human beings, we have the tendency to reciprocate a good deed. But we should not just give for the sake of expecting something in return. Give freely from your heart, and the rewards will be greater.

The act of giving allows joy to flow in your heart. Nothing brightens a day more than seeing the smiles on the faces of the recipients of your generosity and hearing them express their heartfelt gratitude to God because of you.

What you give doesn't necessarily have to be a physical material. It can also be time, effort, talent, service, or even an affectionate feeling.

Just like all things in life, generosity needs to have its boundaries. Be careful not to be *over-generous* as your kindness might be taken advantage of, and some people might abuse your good intentions.

There are those people who will continuously be seeking your assistance. Do what you can to help them, but do not become an *enabler*. It's better to teach them how to solve their problems than to always attend to their needs to find a quick way out. Remember the saying that goes *"Give a man a fish and you'll feed him for a day. Teach him how to fish and he'll feed himself for a lifetime."*

One of the unwritten rules of generosity is that 'you don't blow your own horn'. Don't go about announcing your good deeds to the whole world when it is not necessary. If you really desire to give, do it secretly and in private.

One exception to the rule, for me, is that in the process of trying to get more people to sponsor disadvantaged children in developing countries, it may be necessary to tell them that I am already a sponsor myself, to encourage new sponsorships for those children.

Practising generosity will help you put life in perspective. Given the choice, which one would you like better: being the giver or the recipient of charitable gifts? Being the giver, of course!

If you are the one giving, it means that, at this moment, you are in a better financial position than the recipient, doesn't it?

Financial Legacy

It is about time you began practising generosity and teaching your children the same. In a world that says *"Get all you can, can all you get and sit on the can",* it may not be easy, but it is not impossible.

Spending wisely, saving and giving are all habits that need to be embedded into the lives of our children as a legacy. Would you do it?

Finally ...

As a Money Management Coach, I encourage my clients to make sure they have a Will (*Last Will and Testament*) so that whatever they leave as inheritance for their dependents can, at least, be distributed according to their own wishes and not that of a random Judge.

More importantly than that is the LEGACY they leave. This is something impacted into the lives of others, often from ancestors or predecessors.

What financial legacy are you leaving in your children?

I have used the preceding chapters to highlight life-changing financial wisdom that I got from my father, and I can tell you that I am using the same wisdom to live my life financially, and it is working.

Children are fast learners, and in a weird way, they copy what adults, especially their parents, do. So it should not surprise us that they copy the money patterns or values of their parents as well. You have, consciously or unconsciously, been trained to live at a certain level, standard or in a certain pattern by the way your parents lived their lives.

Even if your parents didn't leave a good financial legacy for you, it does not mean you will not be able to pass the new and better financial habits you have cultivated to your children.

You may be wondering if my father singled me out of all his children to teach me these things. No, he didn't single me out; we just had lots of teaching moments as a family in our house while I was growing up, and every one of my siblings had numerous one-to-one times with our parents. Now that I am a Coach, every experience of my own life comes into play when I deal with the finances of others.

I am a firm believer in the law of sowing and reaping; you always reap what you have sown. Teach your children those good money habits so they won't join the *boomerang culture* and return to live in your spare bedroom when they are supposed to have their own houses.

A man is judged not merely for doing wrong but for not doing right.

Do the right thing and leave a good financial legacy in your loved ones.

Help to improve your children's future by being the best example you can be to them in all areas of life – finances included.

About the Author

Niyi Adeoshun, the Money Management Coach, specialises in inspiring and motivating people to live a life of financial freedom in order to fulfil their God-given life purposes.

Niyi, who is a Budget Coach to many individuals & families, is also an Inspirational/Motivational Speaker on personal finance. He has spoken to audiences all over the UK and currently connects with numerous subscribers through his Money Management Tips newsletter.

His book "***Milestones of Financial Freedom***" has been a blessing to many families all over the world, and testimonies are still coming in as to how it is impacting lives for the better.

Niyi lives with his wife and children in Essex, UK.

Other Books by the Author

If you have enjoyed this book, you may want to check out other books by the author.

<u>**Milestones of Financial Freedom**</u>
(Simples Steps for Conquering Debt and Building Wealth)

<u>**The Price of Financial Freedom**</u>
(3 Essential Steps for Breaking The Cycle of Debt)

<u>**Winning Together**</u>
(A Couple's Guide to Success with Money and Marriage)

<u>**Job Loss, Not Life Loss**</u>
(A Step-by-Step Guide to Emotional, Financial, and Career Recovery)

<u>***Lies We Believe About Money***</u>
(Why Christians Struggle with Wealth—and What God Says) About It

<u>**Joshua, Jordan, and Jericho**</u>
(Reaching Beyond All Obstacles to Your Destiny)

<u>**The Worship Minister**</u>
(Pleasing God as We Fulfil His Call)

<u>**Worship: The God Experience**</u>
(Engaging With The Presence of God Constantly)

Resources

One of the most widely known things that Niyi does is his **Money Management Tips newsletter,** through which he shares nuggets of financial wisdom. Just visit his website at: https://www.niyiadeoshun.com. There is always a special gift waiting for you there.

Niyi loves doing public speaking, and at present, he speaks periodically in his local church and other Christian organisations. His talks are a blend of motivation, humour and common sense using biblical principles on faith, family and finances. He always challenges his audiences to change their attitude to debt and become financially free. People are informed, educated and somehow entertained. To have Niyi speak to your church, group, contact him at: info@niyiadeoshun.com

Niyi coaches people for their debt elimination and total financial freedom. He loves working with people who are determined to fulfil their goals and create the life they really want! It's fun, and wonderful things happen!

You can connect with Niyi through these avenues:

Website: http://www.niyiadeoshun.com/

Email: info@niyiadeoshun.com

X: https://x.com/niyiadeoshun

Facebook:
https://www.facebook.com/MoneyManagementCoach

YouTube Channel:
https://www.youtube.com/c/NiyiAdeoshun